CONFESSIONS

CONFESSIONS
From Domestic Violence Victims to Victors in Christ

Karen R. Lewis

MINISTRY IN WRITING, LLC

Confessions: From Domestic Violence Victims to Victors in Christ
Copyright ©2021 Karen R. Lewis

All rights reserved. This book or any portion thereof may not be reproduced or used in any manner whatsoever without the express written permission of the publisher except for the use of brief quotations in a book review.

Published by: Ministry in Writing, LLC
eBook design by: Ministry in Writing, LLC
www.MinistryinWriting.com

Book cover design by: Rebecacovers

DEDICATION

I dedicate this book to Jesus Christ and every domestic violence victim fighting for freedom.

Contents

Acknowledgements xi
Disclaimer xv
Introduction 1

Victim One 3

Victim Two 9

Victim Three 11

Victim Four 15

Victim Five 21

Victim Six 25

Victim Seven 31

Victim Eight 35

Victim Nine 37

Victim Ten 39

Victim Eleven 43

Victim Twelve 47

Victim Thirteen 51
Victim Fourteen 53
Victims Fifteen 59

My Prayer 61
Donations 63
About the Author 65

ACKNOWLEDGEMENTS

My daughter, Tracy Renee Lewis Anderson Before you were taken away from me, murdered while you were eight months pregnant, you shared parts of your life that I never knew. You told me about things that happened to you as a child that you were always afraid to tell me because you didn't want me to go to jail. You feared that I would go to jail and would no longer be able to raise you and your sister. After your life was taken, it pushed me to become an advocate of domestic violence. I made a vow that I would assist as many victims as possible to escape their abusers. I opened The Angel House to help victims of domestic violence by relocating them to a new state for a fresh start.

My daughter, Rychael Nyree Lewis
Thank you for sharing with me all of the terrible things that happened to you as a child while I was at work. Like your sister, you were terrified to tell me when these things happened because you thought I would go to prison and wouldn't be able to see you or your sister again. Sweetheart, I love you more than you will ever know, and I am so sorry that I wasn't there to defend you and your sister during those dark moments. God has strengthened me to forgive and not seek vengeance. I have handed it all over to Lord. I continue to pray for your mind, heart, and safety every day of my life.

Jupiter Entertainment and Fatal Attraction
I would like to thank you for airing a documentary about my daughter Tracy Renée Lewis Anderson on Fatal Attraction season 8 episode 2 "Left for Dead" which was released on TV ONE February 4, 2019.

**Christian Research and Development Institute Thank you for allowing me to be a student for three years. I not only learned to be a better Christian, but I also managed to graduate as a biblical counselor. As a biblical counselor, I not only help victims get to physical safety, but I also help get them to spiritual safety by leading them to Christ. I teach them to let go and let God take total control of their lives.

To my Heavenly Father

Thank You for accepting me as Your child and allowing me to get to know Jesus Christ as my Lord and Savior. Thank You for filling me with the Holy Spirit to direct my path. I am ever so humble, Father, and I appreciate my journey and every part of my past. I promise to stay focused on You, Lord, every day of my life. Amen.

Special thanks to all the victims who allowed me to share their stories. I thank you for trusting me with telling your truth. I thank God that He has given all of you a fresh new start in life. You no longer hide your past. You have chosen to confess your dark life stories so you can breathe, live, and thrive!!!!! I rejoice with you for the freedom that God has given you. Let your new life begin in the name of Jesus.

DISCLAIMER

Some of the events described in this book are incredibly graphic. Reader discretion is advised. Every story is real, and some names have been changed to protect the privacy of everyone involved.

INTRODUCTION

I write this book of confessions for the many victims I have assisted over the past six years as an advocate of domestic violence. By producing this book, it has helped free many of the victims from their past hurt. These victims now understand that they have survived so that they can thrive in their new lives. It was God that put this book in my heart. I believe God will use this book to help save those currently going through or who have gone through domestic abuse. I write this book of confessions to help free individuals from abuse and to bring them to Christ. As a servant of Christ, I pray that God uses me as He chooses. And as I help others grow, I pray that He helps me grow as well.

VICTIM ONE

I was abused as a child, not by my parents but by other family members. While both of my parents worked, they were considered low-income. They couldn't afford to put me in daycare, so they let different family members watch over me as they worked.

I was only four years old, but I remember getting dropped off at my relative's home like it was yesterday. The adults would make me play in my seven-year-old cousin's room while they were in the front room watching soap operas, smoking, and drinking their Pepsi.

My cousin was very happy to have me play in his room. The first time we had a lot of fun playing with toys, laughing, and we even got to eat breakfast and lunch at the table and chair set in his room. The next time I was there, my cousin wanted to play house and wanted me to clean his closet. Once I opened the closet door, he pushed me in and closed the door behind us. He told me he would take his clothes off and that I needed to take mine off as well so that we could play "husband and wife."

Once our clothes were off, we laid on the closet floor, and he put his finger in my private part. I said, "NO! I don't like this." I began crying, so he put his hand over my mouth, pushed me out of the closet, and called me a cry baby. He told me I better not tell, or I couldn't come into his room and play anymore. The next time I was there while my parents worked, the grown-ups sent me to play in my cousin's room again. He told me we were not going to play house in the closet anymore and that this time we were going to be "kissing cousins." I said okay, and we began to play with his train station again until he pushed me onto my back on the floor. He started laughing and kissing me all over my face. We just laughed and kept on until someone walked into the room. He would always tell whoever walked in the room that I said we were kissing cousins. They would laugh along with us then go back into the front room. After a short time of being kissing cousins, he would pull down his pants and have me kiss his butt. Then he had me pull down my pants, and he would also kiss my butt. On my 5th birthday, my relatives gave me cake and ice cream with a few children on their block while my parents worked. After the children went home, my cousin said he had a new gift for me in his room. When we went into his room, he told me to pull down my pants, and he kissed my butt, and this time he also kissed my private part. I was only five, but it felt good to me. This went on until I was seven years old when my parents had divorced, and my mom now had a new man.

When I was nine years old, my mother had my baby brother. Her new man would often beat her up. By the time I was eleven, he had started touching me on different parts of my body while my mother was at work. He made me promise not to tell, or he would kill my mother. After a while, I found the nerve to ask him to lick my private part. He agreed and taught me to do him as well. One day my mom walked in from work early and found him licking my private part, and she shot and killed him. My little brother and I ended up in the foster care system. When I was fourteen, I learned that my father had gotten killed while trying to rob a liquor store. We got bounced around from one foster home to another, and eventually, my brother and I were separated. I began having sex with the last foster parents I had. Once my foster mother found out that I was having sex with my foster father without her being there, she put me out. It was one week before my eighteenth birthday, and I was now homeless with nowhere to go. I had no idea where my brother was. I went and lived with one of my father's sisters. She got me a job as a dancer at a gentlemen's club. That's where I learned to make money. I began to make enough money to get a studio apartment. Every man I ever got with had to lick my private part, or I wanted nothing else to do with him.

By the time I was twenty-four, I had two children. Their father beat me up, and he made me get on welfare and tell the system that I didn't know who my children's father was. His reason was that I had slept with a few of the guys I met while dancing at the club. He eventually left my kids and me, and his mother took my kids and raised them.

I began drinking, smoking weed, and partying all the time and couldn't hold a job. I couldn't even keep a job as a dancer. I was on a low road until I met a man that managed a motel. He let me work at the hotel as a housekeeper. He had sex with me whenever he wanted and would beat me whenever he thought it was another man in my room. I just couldn't take this life anymore. The last time he beat me, I contacted The Angel House.

I didn't want to leave the state, but I went to the Angel House's support groups. I got a job as a waitress at a family diner, and I accepted Christ at one of my support group meetings.

Now, I attend church faithfully, read my bible daily, and I learned to leave my past behind. Oh, and one of the members at my church has rented me a room in her house. Now, I even have a place to live! I am thankful that I got to know Jesus. I serve Him every day.

VICTIM TWO

I married very young. My husband and I smoked weed and partied every chance we got. Then we began having children. We had three children and were living off welfare while trying to keep up with the fast life. I wanted to be a good mother to our children, so I eventually got a retail job.

My husband's drug habit got worse, and he became very abusive. He even began robbing people and caught several robbery charges. The police showed up at our home regularly for domestic violence. I wasn't calling them; my neighbors were calling as they were tired of us disturbing the neighborhood with our fighting.

The last time he beat me, it was so bad that the state threatened to take my children from me if I didn't press charges against him. His violence against me was endangering the children. I finally pressed charges, and he served ten years in prison.

I divorced him while he was in prison and never had another man in my life near my children. I took my children to see their father whenever he could have visitors. I surrendered my life to the Lord, raised my children in church, and decided that I would keep my mind entirely focused on God.

Once my ex-husband was released from prison into a halfway house, he gave his life to the Lord. He began to pursue me, and we dated for two years. We have become husband and wife again, totally living our lives for the Lord. We both work in different ministries in our church, and all three of our children are saved. To God, be the glory.

VICTIM THREE

My mother had been through a terrible marriage with my father. He had even tried to set our house on fire while my mother and I were inside the home. My mom eventually divorced my father and got with another man when I was about five years old. One year later, they married. While my mom went to work, he was supposed to take care of me. My mother had three children with this man, not knowing that he was abusing me, using me as his sex toy. He made me do all kinds of sex acts on him and myself until I was 14 years old. Meanwhile, we all were attending church as a family every Sunday. My father was in prison, still serving time for trying to burn down the house with us in it, so I couldn't talk to him about what was happening. As I grew older, though, I learned that my father was a child molester himself.

I could no longer take the abuse, so I told one of my church members what my stepfather had been doing to me. She called my mother out of church service and made me tell her what her husband had been doing to me for the last nine years. My stepfather was at home as he didn't attend church service with us that day. My mother never returned home from church with my siblings and me. Instead, our church pastor went to our house and made him confess to what he had been doing to me. The pastor then took him to the nearest police station and made him turn himself in. He served many years in prison for abusing me.

I wanted revenge on my stepfather, so I started performing sex acts on his nieces and my siblings, who were all much younger than me. I even made them do sex acts on each other. I would always tell them that they better not tell anyone, or we would all go to jail.

I barely graduated high school and ended up having three children by three different men, living on welfare, and taking little odd jobs here and there. I was a heavy drinker and smoked all the weed I could handle. I had a very high sex drive, so I had sex with just about any man. I contracted several sexually transmitted diseases. I believe all of this stemmed from the abuse I experienced by my stepfather.

After giving birth to my third child, I decided that I wouldn't be with men anymore. I started having relationships with females. Yes, same-sex relationships. I even moved my female lover into my home, allowing her to look after and bathe my children. My oldest two children are now gay. I am no longer with my female lover, so it's just my youngest child and me in the house.

The woman I was with became very jealous and abusive, so I sought help from a domestic violence agency. Although I refused the agency's help to relocate me out of state, I did one-on-one counseling with Karen Lewis. She helped me accept Jesus Christ and stay faithful to the Lord. She also showed me in the bible where a man shouldn't be with a man and a woman shouldn't be with a woman. God created Adam and Eve for a reason- to reproduce. Please know that man and man can't make a child together just like women can't reproduce together. One thing for sure, Ms. Karen will pull some scripture to help you change your life for the better.

I still have many issues, but I have learned to stay focused on the Word of God. I always pray for complete deliverance from my past. I am learning to trust God fully.

VICTIM FOUR

When I was growing up, my mother was a prostitute, a lady of the night. But she never brought any of her 'Johns' home where my six siblings and I lived. She sometimes would come home to spend a couple of hours with us.

I was eight years old, taking care of my six younger siblings. We were stairsteps in age. The only time we had time with our mother was when she was pregnant. Once she delivered the baby, she would be gone again.

My mother always made sure she was pregnant by a man with seniority working in the factory. That way, she could get good child support and put that man on wage assignment and didn't have to worry about her income.

She knew for sure she had income coming in every week.

As we grew older, we would ask her to spend time with us. I will never forget her response to us- "Look, your child support payments pay the rent and utilities, and I get enough food benefits from the government to provide plenty of food for y'all. You got a roof over your heads and food to eat. So quit asking me to stay home. I have to make money for my clothes, and to keep my hair and nails done, cause your sorry daddies ain't gonna provide for me."

Not one of my mother's children completed high school or did anything with our lives. A couple of us landed in jail for selling drugs on the street, and one of my siblings died from an overdose. All of my siblings had children except me. Once my child support stopped when I turned 18 years old, I had to get a job to continue to stay with my mother.

Just so I could stay, I made my mother believe that I got a job as a server for a mini putt-putt golf course. In reality, that's where I met my first 'John.' I was at the putt-putt golf course with two of my friends when an older guy approached me and asked me out. I was so tickled and excited. I left my friends there, and I went out with him. He took me to a hotel and said this was where he was temporarily living because he had just relocated to the area. When we got to his room, he tried to have sex with me, but I refused and told him that I had never had sex before.

We began kissing, and he asked me, "What if I paid you? Will you have sex with me?" I asked him how much he would pay me, and he pulled out a one-hundred-dollar bill. I put it in my purse, and we had sex. I kept telling him that he was hurting me, and he said it was okay and that it would begin to feel better soon. And it did. After it was over, I cleaned myself up, and he dropped me at my friend's house. I never saw him again.

I began hanging outside of bars to meet older men who would have sex with me and pay me for my time with them. After I had been doing this for five years, a gentleman picked me up one day, and I noticed he looked different from the rest of the guys that I had been sleeping with for money. When we got to the hotel room, he locked the door and put a chair in front of it. He then sat in the chair. Boy did that make me nervous.

He began to ask me questions about why I was living the kind of life I lived. I sat on the floor in front of him, and we talked for six hours. He introduced me to Christ, reached in his briefcase, and gave me a bible as a gift. I had never cried so hard in my life. He promised me I would be alright. We went and had breakfast, and then he gave me a business card to The Angel House as I told him that I didn't want to continue living this life.

I remember contacting The Angel House, and I got an appointment. Ms. Karen Lewis was very friendly, and she showed me different scriptures in the bible about why I should live for Christ. I went to see her every day that week, and I finally said to her that even though I wasn't a victim of domestic violence, I needed help relocating. I wanted to start a fresh new life. Ms. Karen explained that having to raise my siblings was abuse. Even though I was the oldest, I was still a child, and my mother shouldn't have forced me to raise her children.

The Angel House assisted me in relocating to another state. When I arrived in the new state, the shelter helped me stay on course. I attended their church services, which were held in their basement on Sundays. And I went to their bible study during the week. I now live in a low-income housing apartment, and I work part-time at that same shelter that helped me. I also work full-time as a stocker at a nearby grocery store.

I love the Lord unconditionally. I always pay my tithes, and I have disciplined myself to read my bible daily. One thing Ms. Karen told me that I will always remember is that my body is God's temple and that I need to treat my body the same way I would treat God Himself.

VICTIM FIVE

I was a lost soul. My mother was a "junkie" (on crack) all my life. She would allow me and my little sister to drink liquor and smoke weed with her and her crew when we were only nine and seven. She said she did it to keep us out of her way while she and her friends were doing their thing.

I decided to go into the military when I was eighteen, but that didn't work out too well. After two years, I returned home and had two children with one of my mother's ex-boyfriends, who ended up overdosing.

I got with this guy, and I'm so thankful we never had children together. He bullied my son all the time. My children and I moved in with him once my mother passed away. This man was so mean to us, taking my welfare check to get high. It got to the point we had no lights, so he ran an electrical cord through the neighbor's window. The water was eventually turned off, and we had no way to wash up, nor could I cook my children anything to eat. He became very violent toward me in front of my children.

My son told the social worker at his school how we were living, and child protection services took my children away from me. I cried and cried, not knowing what to do. As I watched the news, I heard them talk about The Angel House and how they helped domestic violence victims. They had the phone number of The Angel House at the bottom of the screen. I called that number, and Karen Lewis helped me get my children back and relocated us to another state. I didn't like the shelter I was in, but it was a place for me and my children to be together.

My children started a new school, and my sons' grades went from D's and E's to A's and B's. We had food to eat, and I found a job. After living in that shelter for ninety days, we had to leave. Every day, I stayed at the library once my children got out of school, trying to find a place to live. We had a week before our ninety days were up, and I found a Christian shelter willing to help us. It was 2 hours away, so my children had to change schools.

When we arrived at the new shelter, I found the purple bible that Ms. Karen had given me, and I took it to every bible study I attended. My children are doing very well in school, and I got a job at a college as a housekeeper. And because I work at the college, my classes are free. The shelter found low-income housing for my children and me, and they didn't have to change schools again.

Because Ms. Karen led me to give my life to Christ, I now have full-time employment with benefits, my children are doing well, we live in a nice place, and we always have groceries. My children do their homework and household chores. I am so thankful. We are happy because we now live for Christ Jesus. Jesus is the best thing that could have happened to me.

VICTIM SIX

I was a child who never wanted to listen to my parents. I was having sex with my uncle, my father's brother, since I was fourteen years old. My uncle was thirty-four years old, and I was sixteen when he died in a terrible car accident. I then started having sex with one of my schoolteachers, who later relocated to another state. After I graduated high school, I left home immediately and got a job at an amusement park. They gave me housing while I worked there. I began having sex with some of my co-workers, both male and female. After working there for four years, I was pregnant, and I had no idea who the father was. I had to get on welfare to provide for myself and my new twin babies. I was also able to get into low-income housing.

My neighbor helped me get a job at a fast-food restaurant, where I worked for two years. I met a customer who came into the restaurant, which I dated for a little over a year and married. I don't know why I married him because he only worked at amusement carnivals that traveled around the state. When I started complaining about us not having enough money to take care of a family of four, he began robbing gas stations to help with the household expenses. He told me he was doing janitorial work in the evening, so I never knew he was actually out committing robberies. One day the police showed up at our door and arrested him for robbery. He lied to me, saying that they had him mixed-up with someone else. When I went to his trial, I found out that he had robbed over thirty gas stations. He was sentenced to fifteen years in prison. I was able to get an attorney through legal aid, and I divorced him.

I started dating a guy at my children's school. He worked as a janitor. He had two children, so we often went on playdates whenever his children would visit him. His children were my children's age, so it worked out great. They loved going to the park; we would cook hot dogs and hamburgers and pack snacks in a picnic basket. He ended up losing his apartment and moved in with me. He became very abusive, but I stayed with him for five years. He told me all the time that I was good for nothing and that I would always work at that fast food joint and nobody else would ever want me.

I eventually called the police and had him arrested. I moved in with one of my co-workers and her kids to keep him from finding me. I kept the same job but was able to transfer to another location. I had moved up to the manager position at the new location within six months and was able to get into a new place. My babies loved our new place and were excited about their new school.

Although I was still struggling not knowing which way to turn, the restaurant owner told me that she saw good in me and knew that I could do something more with my life. She knew that I was with a new guy who was abusing me verbally. She gave me the number to The Angel House. I couldn't attend the support groups at The Angel House because it was in another state, but Karen Lewis would talk to me on the phone every week to check on me, and she would always tell me about God. I took her advice and got involved in the church, and I left that verbally abusive guy alone. I also started going to community college to study business. I surrendered to God and graduated from the community college. My boss at the restaurant gave me the downpayment to purchase my own fast food restaurant, and she has been mentoring me ever since.

My children and I are living a much better life now. We now own our own home, and my children's grades have improved so much in school, and they are just as active in church as I am. I now believe the Word of God where it says, "A man that finds a wife finds a good thing." Therefore, I am no longer looking for a man. I am preparing myself to be a good wife to the man that God gives me as a husband.

I now have a very good relationship with my parents and siblings. My children know my family, and they spend time with their grandparents. They are always telling me, "Mommy, thank you for introducing us to our grandparents." They even invited my parents to come to our state to visit us for Thanksgiving.

WOW!! Once I surrendered to God and started living according to His Word, my entire life changed. And I thank God every day.

VICTIM SEVEN

I had just gone through a nasty divorce; my husband left me for a much younger woman. I spent days and nights crying over my ex-husband. All of my friends, including my male friends, urged me to go on with my life. "You are wasting your tears crying over a man who is not crying about you," they said. They reminded me that he moved on with his life and that I needed to do the same. I took their advice but took a different route. I found Jesus and truly fell in love with Him. I found a church for my children and me to attend. We became faithful members and were very active in the church. Four years later, I was informed that the pastor had been having sex with my 16-year-old daughter since she was 12 years old.

I pressed charges, and he was sentenced to

17 years in prison. This caused my daughter to stop talking to me. She didn't want to have anything to do with me. She blamed me for "her man" going to jail, so she ran away repeatedly. Eventually, she moved in with one of our relatives until she turned eighteen and got an apartment with one of her friends. It's been fifteen years, and my daughter still wants nothing to do with me or her siblings.

I pray for my daughter daily to seek a relationship with God and understand that I did what was best for her. I pray she will understand what that pastor did was wrong. I also pray that the pastor asks God for forgiveness if he hasn't already.

I lost my ex-husband and my child, but I never gave up on Jesus. My life sounds like a sad story, but I realize God still loves me no matter what. I used to tell myself daily that I was a bad mother because I didn't protect my daughter from that pastor. But God showed me through my other two children that I was a very good mother.

I heard about a lady named Karen Lewis and

how she always prayed for her victims. I reached out to her, and she always made time to listen and pray for me. We are not in the same state, so our communication is long-distance. I have been getting biblical counseling from her for four years now. I have yet to meet her in person, but I have a spiritual connection with her. She tells me all the time to keep telling my story because it might help someone. Karen also prays with me for my daughter to return so that we will all be united again.

I am so thankful for the strength of my children, who held me up in prayer when I thought I couldn't make it anymore. My children still tell me that they are glad that I didn't give up on Jesus.

I am so thankful that my children continue to serve God and still love me. Thank you, Jesus!

VICTIM EIGHT

Thank God for The Angel House. I had two children with two different men who were both very abusive. One day my youngest child's father beat me to no end and threatened to kill my parents if I didn't come back to him. It had gotten so bad that my parents retired and moved to another state. I went to The Angel House with my children and was relocated to another state to begin a fresh new life.

After two years of being free, I received a letter from the courts stating that I was an unfit mother, and if I didn't return my oldest child to the state where his father resided, they would be pressing charges against me. My 12-year-old son told me that he had been keeping in touch with his father, and he said he wanted to go live with him.

I had to travel back to my former state for a custody hearing. The judge granted 50/50 custody of my son to his father and me. So, we would meet at the halfway mark between the states in which we resided. That following year, my son's father went to prison for domestic violence and drug charges. I went back before that same judge, and this time, I got full custody. I am now married to a God-fearing man and pregnant with our first child together.

VICTIM NINE

I met my wife in college. She was very physically abusive toward me, and many times I tried to stop seeing her, but she would always give me a sad story, and we'd make up. During our last fight, she hit me on my back with the hot iron she was using to iron her work uniform. I decided then that we would never see each other again.

A month later, she informed me that she was eight weeks pregnant with our child. I let her know that we could co-parent, but we would never be together again. She began writing me letters stating that she was going to The Angel House for domestic violence counseling, trying to become a better person.

I attended prenatal appointments with her until she gave birth to our beautiful daughter.

One of the nurses talked to us about God before she was discharged. We started to go to church together, and we began dating again.

Four years later, we are now married with two children, and she still attends group sessions with The Angel House.

What I am saying is that prayer works, and counseling works. There is no abuse in our home, only the love of God.

We will be moving out of state soon, but Karen Lewis says that she will continue to counsel my wife by phone. This way, my wife will be able to help others in our new state. What a blessing.

VICTIM TEN

My husband and I had been attending church together since we got married. We raised three daughters together, and then I finally left him after 17 years of marriage. He was very abusive with our finances and the way he talked to me. He always wanted to control me. We owned our own construction business, and I did all of the paperwork, but he only paid me one hundred dollars per week. I had to ask for grocery money and money to buy the children's clothes and school supplies.

We tried going to marriage counseling, but our church's pastors weren't feeling me at all. They told me that this is the life that my husband had chosen for us; therefore, I had to be obedient. I was shocked to hear this from my pastor and First Lady. I took that as a lesson learned, and from that moment, I knew I was at the wrong church. I did not want my daughters growing up believing that.

Someone told me about The Angel House, so I started to attend their support groups. My husband worked overtime, and he would think I was at the grocery store. I learned from my group sessions that verbal, financial, and emotional abuse is just as bad as physical abuse.

I didn't want to relocate out of state, so I made my own escape plan. I took a personal loan from the bank using the business account, moved eight cities away from my husband while he was at work, and started a new job. My daughters were happier than I was. My youngest daughter told me she had been praying that we would move away from their father, which made me very sad.

I am now living a stress-free life. I own a townhouse, a car in my name, I have a job, and my daughters are happy most of all. We even found a lovely church home. I am so glad that I never took my eyes off God. I will continue to pray and praise the Lord.

VICTIM ELEVEN

I have been a victim all my life, and I still don't have a success story yet. My prayer to God is if I never have a success story, at least let one of my six children have a success story. As a child, my mother was a junkie. I was the oldest of 6; I had one sister and four brothers. I was the one she picked to sell so she could get her drugs. I had two children by the time I was fifteen and didn't know who their fathers were. I could barely keep them fed and clothed because I was on my mother's welfare case, and she wasn't giving me any money. I could only feed them what the neighbors would give me. Some of my neighbors even gave me clothes for both my children and me.

My grandparents finally decided to take my children and me in to live with them. But by this time, I enjoyed having sex, so I ended up with four children at age eighteen. My grandparents couldn't handle me having babies, so my grandfather brought me a three-bedroom home on a land contract. The house didn't have a basement, but it did have a laundry room, which I made into a bedroom. I decided to just go to a laundromat to do my laundry. When I was twenty, I had six children and had to have a hysterectomy because I had caught so many sexually transmitted diseases.

My grandparents died in a car accident, and I couldn't keep up with the land contract payments, so I lost my house. The state assisted me with getting a new place. I never finished school, and I had no job skills, but I had to work to keep my welfare benefits. I got a job cleaning up in a laundromat, but I used most of that money to buy liquor. I had become an alcoholic.

The county watched my kids while I worked, but my life wasn't getting any better, and I didn't care. I thought I loved my children, but I wasn't sure. As long as I had a man in my life and liquor to drink, I was fine. I made sure my children had cereal, lunch meat, bread, and milk with the food benefits I received every month. As long as they didn't run out of food, that was good enough for me.

Once I turned thirty, my oldest child was seventeen, and he was in and out of youth prison for selling drugs on the streets. I started working at a janitorial cleaning company making a little more money, but all my children were doing terrible in school. I could barely read myself, so I couldn't help them. By the time I turned forty, I was in prison. I had driven the getaway car while a friend of mine robbed a gas station for liquor, money, and cigarettes, which was all caught on camera. As I sat in prison, another inmate shared information about the Angel House and asked if it was okay if she shared my name and inmate number with Karen Lewis, owner of The Angel House. I agreed, and to this day, Ms. Karen keeps in touch with me. She faithfully sends me letters of hope, prayers, and encouragement. She knows that none of my children ever finished school and that three are also in prison, and the state has most of my grandchildren. This lady is amazing. She has built relationships with my other three children, assisting them in getting into programs that will advance their lives. I couldn't help my children, but God put someone in our lives that could tell us about the goodness of God and prays for us all the time. As I continue to sit in prison, I pray that God will bless Karen Lewis and allow her to continue to help others as she's helping my family and me.

VICTIM TWELVE

My life was shattered when I met this lady. She was about my age, and I had been complaining to her about every area of my life. I told her how my brothers, who were younger than me, sexually assaulted me all my life and how my mother allowed it. I would come home from school and hide in my bedroom closet so they wouldn't know I was home.

I realize now that my mother had mental issues, which is why she allowed my brothers to do those awful things to me. One of my brothers broke my jaw because I refused to have sex with him. I had to go to the hospital, and my mother dared me to tell the doctors what my brothers had been doing to me. My parents divorced when I was nine years old, and my mother hated me ever since. She hated me because I looked so much like my father, who had left her alone with eight children.

Once they divorced, I had to become the head of the household. My mother refused to do anything else for us. Even with my brothers attacking me, I still had to cook, clean, and bathe my youngest siblings. When I was old enough to get a job, I gave my little sisters money to buy groceries to cook once I got off work.

At 19 years old, I moved out and got my own place. My siblings often cried to me because they were always without food. I would help them when I could. I dropped out of school because I thought people knew how I was living, and I was embarrassed. As I complained every day at work, this lady finally told me of her past struggles and how she serves God. I got to know her better, and every time I tried to complain, she reminded me that I am still living today. She encouraged me to share my story with others because I never knew who

I would be helping. That lady is Karen Lewis, the founder of The Angel House. She gives motivation and encouragement to everyone she encounters. Lord, please continue to bless Ms. Karen so that she blesses and encourages others. She deserves it.

VICTIM THIRTEEN

I moved from Michigan to Tennessee and then to Florida and back to Michigan, trying to escape my abuser. Now I am in a new state far away, thanks to The Angel House. I don't want to say too much about my story. Still, everyone needs to know that The Angel House is an underground organization that genuinely helps victims of domestic violence escape their abusers so we can get a fresh new start in life. All three of my children are grown, now living their own lives. One of my sons became an abuser, just like his dad, and wants nothing to do with me because I helped his wife and children get away from him. My abuser later died at the hands of one of his victims, who killed him in self-defense. I am doing just fine, although I continue to see a therapist. I just want to say thank you, Karen Lewis, for assisting me. I pray that you will continue to help other victims.

VICTIM FOURTEEN

I had to go to The Angel House for help because I had gotten myself into a twisted situation. I got involved with this young man when I was eighteen. My mother had just died, and I was an only child who didn't know many of my relatives.

Nothing was right about this man, but I ended up having five children with him. I lived in Section 8 housing because he didn't believe in working, and he would always tell me I could live off the system just like his mama did.

I learned how to braid hair when I was very young, so I used hair braiding to make money. This was how I was able to take care of my children as he used our welfare money to get high and buy beer. Every month when my food benefits were loaded on my EBT card, he would take me to the grocery store and allow me to purchase peanut butter & jelly, bread, cereal, and sometimes lunch meat. I was also able to buy two gallons of milk because I was receiving WIC. He said I needed to learn how to season canned beef, pork, and chicken so my kids could have a "good meal" every day.

I was so involved in the street that he moved this girlfriend in with us. She had two children, which I ended up having to take care of as if they were my own. The three of us slept in the same bed, and he made us have sex in ways I never imagined. He made me and the other woman get each other's names tattooed on our arms and butt. He also performed what he called a marriage ceremony between the three of us in the bedroom. He had us all prick our fingers and mix our blood. He then pronounced us husband and wives.

He said that since we were all married, I had to give the other woman half my income from braiding hair and keep gas in his car. Once he and the other woman got very close, he began beating me in front of my children. One time he beat me so bad I ended up in the hospital.

The nursing assistant recognized me and asked if I was Annie's daughter. I told him yes and that she had been dead for ten years. He was shocked and told me his brother was my father. The next day my father visited me in the hospital, and he was disabled, bound to a wheelchair. We talked for hours. He told me he left my mom when I was four months old because she was sleeping with his best friend. When he had confronted them, his best friend shot him, which caused him to become permanently disabled. The best friend went to jail for shooting my father, and my mother went on with her life. They had grown up in the same neighborhood and knew some of the same people, and they would always tell him how I was doing. He said that my mom got a social security check for me since he was receiving one due to not working. He also told me that he never visited me because he didn't want me to see him like that.

When I got out of the hospital, my father took me to my house to pick up my kids so we could stay with him until I could get back on my feet. While at my house, my children's father threatened my father and began beating him very badly. A neighbor called the police because my father couldn't defend himself.

Once the police came and arrested my children's father, we left the other woman and her two children in that house. When he was released from jail, he started threatening me. He had a tracker on my phone, so we drove a couple of cities away and threw the phone out the car window. We stayed at a hotel in the next state over, and this was when I learned about the Angel House.

I contacted The Angel House, and Ms. Lewis was able to assist my family and me. We are safe in a state far away from my abuser, and because my dad had income, they were able to find housing for us immediately. We stayed in the shelter for three days before moving into our new home. I got a job in a hair salon braiding hair, and my father watches my children while I work and attend night school.

I am so grateful that we met Ms. Lewis. She helped us find a church home in our new state, which we attend regularly. My dad and I have accepted Jesus Christ as our Lord and Savior. We are both very active at church, and my children even love attending. We have a long way to go, but God is with us every step of the way.

VICTIMS FIFTEEN

My parents were married for thirty-seven years, and both had cushion jobs at their place of employment. They grew up in the same neighborhood, finished high school, went to college together, and had two children. They had a daughter first, and two years later, they had me- their son. They were totally in love. Then in 2019, at the age of thirty-two, I received a text message from my mother with a picture. She had walked from the building that she worked in across to the building my father worked in. When she opened the door to his office, he was having sex with another woman. My mother had sent the picture to both my sister and me with a text that said,

"This is why I am no longer with you." She then committed suicide. My mother was very good friends with the founder of The Angel House, Ms. Karen Lewis. Ms. Lewis has helped both me and my sister deal with our mother's loss, and she also provides excellent resources for our therapy.

My sister and I see a different therapist because we feel we can get better help this way. We still don't communicate with our father, but maybe one day, with both of us accepting Christ as our Savior, we will. I have no children, but my sister is married with three children, and she doesn't allow them to see our father. It's been very hard on both of us, and I pray to Jesus every day that he will remove this anger from my sister and me. Thank you, Ms. Karen Lewis, for everything. You have taught us that we don't have to be messed up for life. We have Jesus.

My Prayer

Father, I pray that each of these victims will walk with you for the rest of their lives and that they understand how important it is to tell the world about their past traumas. They may never know who they are helping. Lord, let these victims know that they are now free to serve You, Father. I pray nothing but success over every victim's life that has reached out to The Angel House.

Lord see to it that The Angel House receives daily donations so we can continue to help victims like the ones who shared their stories in this book. In the name of Jesus. Amen.

Donations

Donations can be made to The Angel House.

Online: www.theangelhouse.org
Cash app: $KRAT3
Mail: 33228 West 12 Mile Road, Farmington Hill, Michigan 48334

Please note: The Angel House is not a shelter. We are an underground organization that helps victims escape their abusers by bus, train, or plane. Our goal is to get them to safety to begin a fresh new life. Thank you for taking the time to read this book, and please share it with everyone you know. God bless you.

About the Author

Karen R. Lewis was born and raised in Detroit, Michigan, where she still resides. She raised her two beautiful daughters in Michigan as well. She worked for the State of Michigan for twenty-three years. Karen was a victim of domestic violence for thirteen years by her former husband. She thought because she left her husband when her children were four and seven years of age, her daughters would never experience domestic violence. Once she received the news that her youngest daughter, Tracy Renee, who was eight months pregnant, was murdered, stabbed fifty-six times by her abuser on March 21, 2014, she was devastated. She retired from the State of Michigan due to the grief she suffered.

Karen is the founder of **The Angel House,**

an organization she started after losing her daughter to this horrific act. Karen became an advocate for domestic violence victims in 2014 and has vowed to help every victim she can for the rest of her life. She asks people, organizations, businesses, and companies for monetary donations every day, so she will always be able to purchase bus, train, or plane tickets for victims to escape their abusers and start a fresh new life.

Karen graduated from Christian Research and Development Institute as a Christian Biblical Counselor on July 19, 2010. She also received her certification as a hospital chaplain from the Healthcare Christian Fellowship of Michigan in August 2017. She then returned to Healthcare Christian Fellowship of Michigan and received her certification as an Evangelist in November 2019. Karen is consistently bringing awareness to domestic violence through speaking engagements to prevent women and their children from becoming statistics of this growing crime. She assists victims of domestic violence in hopes that the victims will learn about God and live according to His Word.

Made in the USA
Columbia, SC
06 June 2022